Julia Greeley

Under the direction of Romain Lizé, CEO, MAGNIFICAT
Editor, MAGNIFICAT: Isabelle Galmiche
Editor, Ignatius: Vivian Dudro
Proofreader: Kathleen Hollenbeck
Layout Designer: Gauthier Delauné
Production: Thierry Dubus, Audrey Bord

MAURA ROAN MCKEEGAN • GINA CAPALDI

Julia Greeley

Secret Angel to the Poor

MAGNIFICAT · Ignatius

An old woman with a floppy hat and flapping shoes hobbled down the street, pulling a little red wagon behind her.

In the wagon were a sack of potatoes, a pile of children's coats, and a patched-up old doll.

The old woman pulled her wagon up to the fire station. Two firemen were coming out the door, heading for home after working the night shift. They waved as soon as they saw her.

"Miss Julia!" the first fireman said. "What brings you here so early?"

Julia smiled. "The good Lord has work for me to do today, Mr. James, and it is my joy to do it." She showed them a handful of coins. "I'd like to buy some coal, but I'm short on change. I'd be obliged if you could help."

Both firemen reached into their pockets without hesitation and emptied their change into Julia's open hands.

"Anything to see you smile, Miss Julia," the second fireman said.

"Thank you, gentlemen," Julia said with a grin. She put the money safely into her big black handbag, then pressed into each fireman's hand a small badge with a picture of a crowned heart printed on it. "May the Sacred Heart of Jesus reward you for your kindness."

Miss Julia pulled her wagon along until she reached the steps of Sacred Heart Church. The parish priest was coming up the sidewalk.

"Morning, Miss Julia," he said, glancing into the wagon. "That's a nice doll. Who's it for?"

"I found it in the road last week, Father Barry," Julia answered. "It was badly broken. I brought it home and fixed it up, so I can give it to a little girl I know."

She parked her wagon beneath an oak tree and climbed the steps to enter the church, just as she did every morning. As she went to kneel in the front pew, two ladies approached Father Barry in the back of the church.

"Father, I'm concerned about Old Julia," one of them said in a low voice.

"What do you mean?" Father Barry asked.

"Well, last night, I looked out my window, and I saw her walking down my street. I could hardly believe what I was seeing. It was pitch dark, and she was carrying a *mattress* on her back!"

"It's all very strange, Father," the second woman broke in. "She pulls that little red wagon everywhere, collecting old things. She has that dreadful-looking eye. And she's here at Mass every morning, right in the front pew. Can't you make her sit in the back?"

"As long as I'm pastor here, Julia is going to keep her pew," Father Barry replied sternly. "She can sit any place she wants. And while she might look dreadful to you–to me, she has the face of an angel. Do you want to know how her eye was injured?"

"I heard it was some sort of accident," the first woman answered.

"It was no accident," Father Barry replied. "A slave owner's whip hit her in the eye when she was just a child."

Father Barry looked over at Julia. Her head was bowed in prayer, and her hands clasped the beads of a rosary. "That's right," the priest continued. "She grew up in slavery. She wasn't allowed to learn to read and write. Yet she is more knowledgeable in the ways of God than anyone I've ever known. To tell you the truth," he said, his eyes still fixed on her, "I believe that woman is a saint."

The women followed his gaze over to Julia.

"And that mattress she was carrying on her back last night came from me," the priest said. "She asked me for it yesterday, and I gave it to her from an extra bed in the rectory. A poor old man was sick, and he had no bed. Julia wanted him to have a comfortable place to rest."

Father Barry cleared his throat and nodded slightly. "If you'll excuse me, I have to get ready for Mass."

He left the women standing in the back of the church, watching Julia. She didn't look like any saint they had ever seen. But they didn't yet know the greatness of her love. They didn't know that she had heard every word they had said or that as they watched her now, she was asking Jesus to forgive them and to help them know the love of his Sacred Heart.

ater that morning, Julia knocked on the door of a large, white house. A woman with a kind face opened the door and smiled. She was holding a baby.

"Thank goodness you're here!" she said, placing the baby into Julia's open arms. "I have to run out to the store, but I know I can trust you to watch my little Marjorie while I'm gone."

"I'll take good care of her, Mrs. Agnes," Julia said, smiling like an angel at the little girl she held. Marjorie put her arms around the old woman and kissed her cheeks.

"She's a lot happier now that you're here," Mrs. Agnes said. "I don't know what we'd do without you, Miss Julia." She reached behind the door and wheeled out a baby carriage. "Here, you can take her for a walk in this new buggy. We just bought it yesterday!"

"It's lovely, ma'am," Julia said, nodding her head thoughtfully. She looked at the old buggy sitting in a corner by the door. "Mrs. Agnes, if it's not too much to ask, may I have the old one?"

The young mother laughed. "By all means; do whatever you'd like with it. Here, take some fruit with you, too," she added, stuffing several apples and oranges into Julia's big black handbag.

"Thank you, ma'am," Julia said, as she handed baby Marjorie her rosary beads, which she often used to teach the little girl to pray. "May the Sacred Heart of Jesus reward you for your kindness."

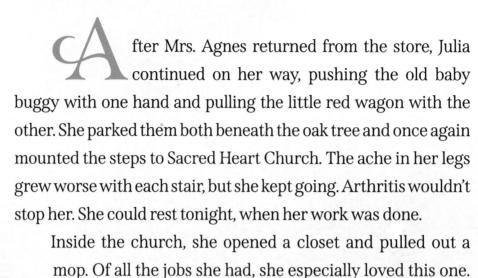

After Mrs. Agnes returned from the store, Julia continued on her way, pushing the old baby buggy with one hand and pulling the little red wagon with the other. She parked them both beneath the oak tree and once again mounted the steps to Sacred Heart Church. The ache in her legs grew worse with each stair, but she kept going. Arthritis wouldn't stop her. She could rest tonight, when her work was done.

Inside the church, she opened a closet and pulled out a mop. Of all the jobs she had, she especially loved this one. It filled her with joy to make the church shine for Jesus. It was a gift she could offer his Sacred Heart.

As she mopped, Julia noticed a woman in the pews. The woman held her head in her hands and tears rolled down her cheeks. She didn't see Julia.

"Lord, our house is so cold," she wept. "Please help me keep my children warm."

The woman had no idea that someone mopping the floor behind her had overheard her prayer.

Old Julia had a way of hearing things, whenever someone was in need.

When she finished cleaning the church, Julia pulled her little red wagon over to the next block. She stopped in front of a group of children singing and dancing in the street.

"Miss Julia!" a little boy called, waving at her. "Want to join us?"

"Sure, sonny," the old woman replied. The next minute, she was holding up the sides of her long skirt, singing and dancing and laughing with the children.

When the song was over, the children gathered around her as she opened her big black handbag. "Let's see, an apple for you, an orange for you," she said, giving each child a piece of fruit.

One little boy plunged his teeth into his apple ravenously. Julia watched him consume it in giant bites, like a hungry wolf.

"Petey, have you eaten anything today?" she asked.

Petey shook his head. "Mama says we can't have nothin' to eat until suppertime, 'cause the cupboard's almost bare."

"Here, child, have my last apple." Julia pulled the apple from her handbag and put it into Petey's eager hands. "Which one is your house again?" she asked him. Still chewing, the boy pointed to a house across the street, and Julia nodded.

T hen Julia looked around, searching for a particular face.

"Where's Anna?" she asked.

"Over there," a boy said, pointing to a porch where a little girl sat alone.

Julia pulled the wagon over and knelt beside her.

"How's my Anna today?" she asked, taking the girl's hand.

The girl tried to answer, but she began sobbing instead.

"Bless your little heart, child," Julia said, hugging her. "I know things haven't been the same since your mama died. Look, I brought you something." She took the doll from the wagon and placed it in the girl's lap.

Anna's eyes grew wide and her sobs quieted as she looked at the doll. "Th-thank you," she whispered. Tenderly she picked up the doll, closing her eyes and rocking it as if all that remained in the world were herself and the doll.

Julia stood up and patted the girl's head. Humming a hymn to the Sacred Heart, she went on her way.

Late that night, an old woman with a floppy hat and flapping shoes pulled a little red wagon and a baby carriage through a dark alley.

A young boy was running up his front steps when he heard the wagon wheels rattle. He turned around and watched the old woman as she drew near. Their eyes met.

"Here, sonny," Julia whispered. "Do a favor for Old Julia. See that house right there? I left some potatoes on the back porch. I'm afraid they'll freeze and spoil if no one sees them there. If you would be good enough to help, run up onto the porch, give a knock, and run away. And don't dare say Old Julia sent you."

The boy knew Old Julia. She had given his family firewood last month, when his father had hurt his back. All the children in the neighborhood would do anything Julia asked, and this boy was no different.

He ran up to his neighbor's porch where the potatoes were, knocked on the door, and ran off, while Julia wheeled her wagon back down the dark alley. It wasn't the safest way to go, but it was the most hidden. She didn't want to embarrass people by bringing charity to their doorsteps in the daylight. That's why she always made her deliveries at night.

An hour later, Julia told her tired legs to keep going just a little longer. Soon she would be at her boarding house, where she could sleep for a few hours before Mass in the morning. But first, she had more deliveries to make.

She had just put the buggy on the porch of a mother who was going to have her first baby any day now. Now she had only a bucket of coal and a pile of children's coats left in her wagon. It was a good thing those firemen had helped her buy the coal this morning. Good thing she had these coats, too. Only yesterday, a family whose children had outgrown them had offered them to her while she was walking by their house. God knew she would need them tonight.

Julia parked the wagon outside of a small house. She took out the bucket of coal. It was heavy, but she managed to haul it quietly onto the doorstep. Then she returned to her wagon for the coats, which she laid beside the coal. Her sore feet stumbled a bit as she left, and she hoped no one heard her.

Inside the little house, someone quickly lit a lamp. A woman opened the door and looked around, but she saw no one.

Shivering with cold, she stepped out on the porch. When she saw the gifts on her doorstep, she fell to her knees. She didn't know who had brought the coal that would heat her house and the beautiful warm coats for her little ones. But she knew that God had answered her prayer—the one she had prayed in Sacred Heart Church that very afternoon.

He would keep her family warm.

The next morning, Julia pulled her little red wagon toward the steps of Sacred Heart Church. Outside, two women were talking. Julia saw that they were the same women who had approached Father Barry in the back of the church the day before.

"You wouldn't believe it," the first woman was saying. "Just yesterday, I was inside the church, begging God to help me keep my children warm. And last night, I found a bucket of coal and a pile of children's coats on my doorstep."

"You found gifts on your porch, too?" her friend asked in surprise. Then her voice shook with emotion. "My husband has been out of work," she confided. "We couldn't even give the children a meal until suppertime yesterday. Our cupboard was almost bare. We were about to go to bed when I heard a knock at the door. When I went out, no one was there, but a big bag of potatoes was sitting on my back porch. It's as if an angel left it there. I came back here to thank God."

Julia parked her wagon under the oak tree and walked past the women, up the steps. She kept her eyes down, until one of them called her name.

"'Mornin', Miss Julia," the first woman said. She had been doing a lot of thinking after talking to Father Barry the previous morning, and she had decided that maybe she had been wrong about Julia. Perhaps she should get to know this interesting woman Father Barry believed was a saint.

ulia's face broke into a big smile as she lifted her eyes and looked at the woman. "'Mornin', ma'am," she replied, nodding as she opened the door and entered the church.

"I must say, there is something beautiful in that woman's smile," the second woman said to her friend as they climbed the steps behind her.

"Miss Julia," Mrs. Agnes asked later that day, when Julia had finished cleaning the house and watching Marjorie. "When is your birthday? We'd like to get you some new things, so you don't have to keep asking for so many old ones."

"My birthday, ma'am? I reckon I don't believe I know. I never was told."

Mrs. Agnes was stunned. "You don't know how old you are?"

"No, ma'am," Julia answered.

"No one ever gave you birthday presents?"

"No, ma'am," replied Julia. "But I've not needed any. The good Lord gives me all I need."

As she hugged Marjorie goodbye, Julia caught sight of an old blanket hanging on a hook by the door. "Mrs. Agnes," she said, nodding toward the hooks. "That blanket Marjorie never uses anymore—may I have it?"

"For you, Julia," Mrs. Agnes said, taking the blanket and wrapping it around Julia's shoulders, "anything. I hope it keeps you warm."

"Oh, it's not for me, ma'am," Julia said. "The fire of the Sacred Heart of Jesus keeps me warm. The Lord needs this for someone else."

Julia limped down the front steps and put the blanket in her wagon alongside a loaf of bread and a load of firewood.

"May the Sacred Heart of Jesus reward you for your kindness," she called to the young mother, who stood on the porch with her baby, watching Julia leave.

The old woman shuffled off down the street, pulling her little red wagon behind her.

Background to This Story

- Julia Greeley was born into slavery and later freed.

- She didn't know how old she was.

- Since slaves were forbidden to read and write, Julia was mostly illiterate.

- Her right eye was injured by a slave owner when she was a child.

- People called her—and she called herself—"Old Julia."

- She limped from severe arthritis.

- She wore a big, black floppy hat and shoes that flapped when she walked.

- Her parish was Sacred Heart, where she went to Mass every morning.

- The priests at Sacred Heart helped Julia with her charitable works.

- One priest who supported Julia was named Fr. Edward Barry. When some women complained to him about her sitting in the front pew, he defended her with the words used in this book: "As long as I'm pastor here, Julia is going to keep her pew."

- Although very poor herself, Julia spent most of her money buying things she knew others needed. What she couldn't buy, she begged for.

- She pulled a little red wagon filled with food, fuel, and clothing for the poor, and she made her deliveries at night so that families wouldn't be embarrassed.

- Julia was once seen on the streets at night carrying a mattress on her back.

- She asked people to donate their old baby buggies for poor families.

- Her employment consisted of cleaning houses and taking care of children. She also cleaned the church.

- She worked for a woman named Agnes Urquhart and cared for her daughter, Marjorie. Julia taught baby Marjorie to pray on her rosary beads. Agnes gave donations to Julia's charitable collections.

- Julia once comforted and cared for a little girl who lost her mother.

- Some people were startled at the sight of Julia, especially because of her eye, but her charity made them forget her appearance. They said her smile was beautiful and unforgettable.

- If Julia received apples, oranges, or other gifts at one house, she would put them in her big black handbag and distribute them to the next people on her rounds.

- She loved children, delighted in giving them gifts, fixed up broken dolls for them, and was known to pick up the sides of her long skirt and join the children as they sang and danced and laughed in the streets.

- She had a fervent devotion to the Sacred Heart. As she worked, she prayed and sang hymns to the Sacred Heart.

- She regularly visited Denver's firefighters, and gave them Sacred Heart badges, and they supported her charitable collections.

- She once asked a boy to knock on the door of a house where she had left potatoes so that they wouldn't freeze and spoil overnight. She told him not to dare say Old Julia had sent him.

Postscript

This fictionalized story is based on true events in the life of Julia Greeley, who was born sometime between 1833 and 1848. (She never knew her birthday.)

After so many years of pouring out her life for the love of Jesus, Julia fell ill on her way to First Friday Mass on June 7, 1918—the feast of the Sacred Heart—and was taken to the hospital. She died that night. Since she had no known relatives, the parish priests arranged her funeral.

When her viewing was held at Sacred Heart Church, huge crowds lined up for hours to honor her. Only then did people begin to realize how many lives she had touched with her humble charity and secret deliveries.

Her cause for sainthood was introduced in 2016.

Acknowledgements and many thanks to Fr. Blaine Burkey, O.F.M. Cap., whose book, In Secret Service of the Sacred Heart: The Life and Virtues of Julia Greeley, *is the source for this biography.*

Printed in June 2022 by Dimograf, Poland

Job number MGN 22020

Printed in compliance with the Consumer Protection Safety Act, 2008